Meet the Cephalopods

Octopus • Squid • Cuttlefish • Nautilus

Celia Svedhem

Illustrated by Filippa Widlund

Translated by B.J. Woodstein

ORCA BOOK PUBLISHERS

Are octopuses aliens? Are squids monsters who live in the seas? Will cuttlefish take over the world?

For centuries, people have been scared of cephalopods such as octopuses, squids, cuttlefish and nautiluses. Could that be because we've known so little about them? Or because they seem so different from us?

Because people didn't know much about them, they made up all sorts of horrible stories. If a ship sank out at sea, folks said a giant squid had wrapped its long tentacles around the ship and dragged it down to the bottom.

But with more advanced technology, scientists in recent years have learned more about cephalopods. For example, octopuses and squids have three hearts and blue blood.

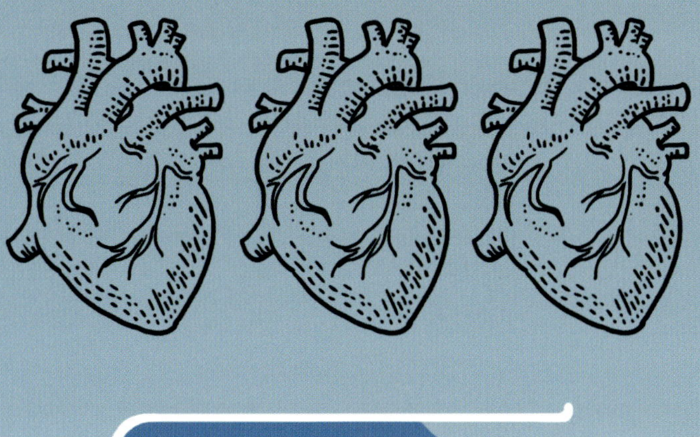

A cephalopod's brain isn't located just in its head, like it is for us, but is spread throughout its whole body.

Though nautiluses have shells, they and other cephalopods don't have skeletons, so their bodies are soft and jellylike. That means they can squeeze through almost any little hole, and some are real escape artists!

DO YOU WANT TO KNOW MORE?

Stick with us now to find out what scientists know about cephalopods. You'll also get to read about some exciting interactions people have had with cephalopods. There's nothing here that people have made up, only things that have actually happened.

Octopus is the name for eight-limbed cephalopods. The 10-limbed cephalopods include squid and cuttlefish. Nautiluses have up to 90 tentacles.

Inky the Octopus

At the National Aquarium of New Zealand, the lid of the octopus tank was accidentally left slightly ajar one night. Inky pushed up an arm, played with the lid a little and squeezed his whole body through the tiny space. Then he slithered down to the floor, crawled about 13 feet (4 meters) to a drainpipe and sneaked into it. He followed the pipe all the way out to the sea—and he became a free octopus again!

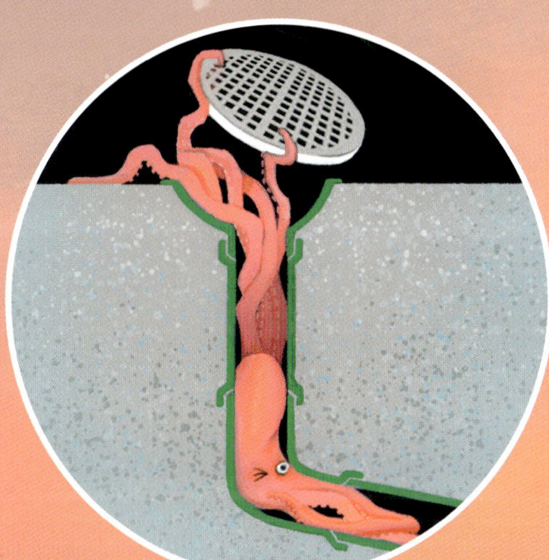

Imagine how surprised Inky's handlers must have been when they got to work the next morning!

Inky's escape became big news, and a reporter asked the staff at the National Aquarium why they thought he had left. They said Inky was at the age when octopuses usually have children, and maybe he was looking for a female to mate with.

But octopuses are smart animals who always want challenges and new things to explore, so maybe he ran away just because he was bored.

Octopuses can live to be five years old, but most live for only two to three years. So it's not strange that Inky didn't want to stay in a little aquarium all day long but wanted to take the opportunity to see the world!

Eight-Limbed Octopus

Cephalopods can be divided into three main groups: the eight-limbed octopuses, the 10-limbed squid and cuttlefish, and the nautiluses. Most people have heard of octopuses. They are the easiest ones for humans to catch sight of, and they are the ones researchers know the most about.

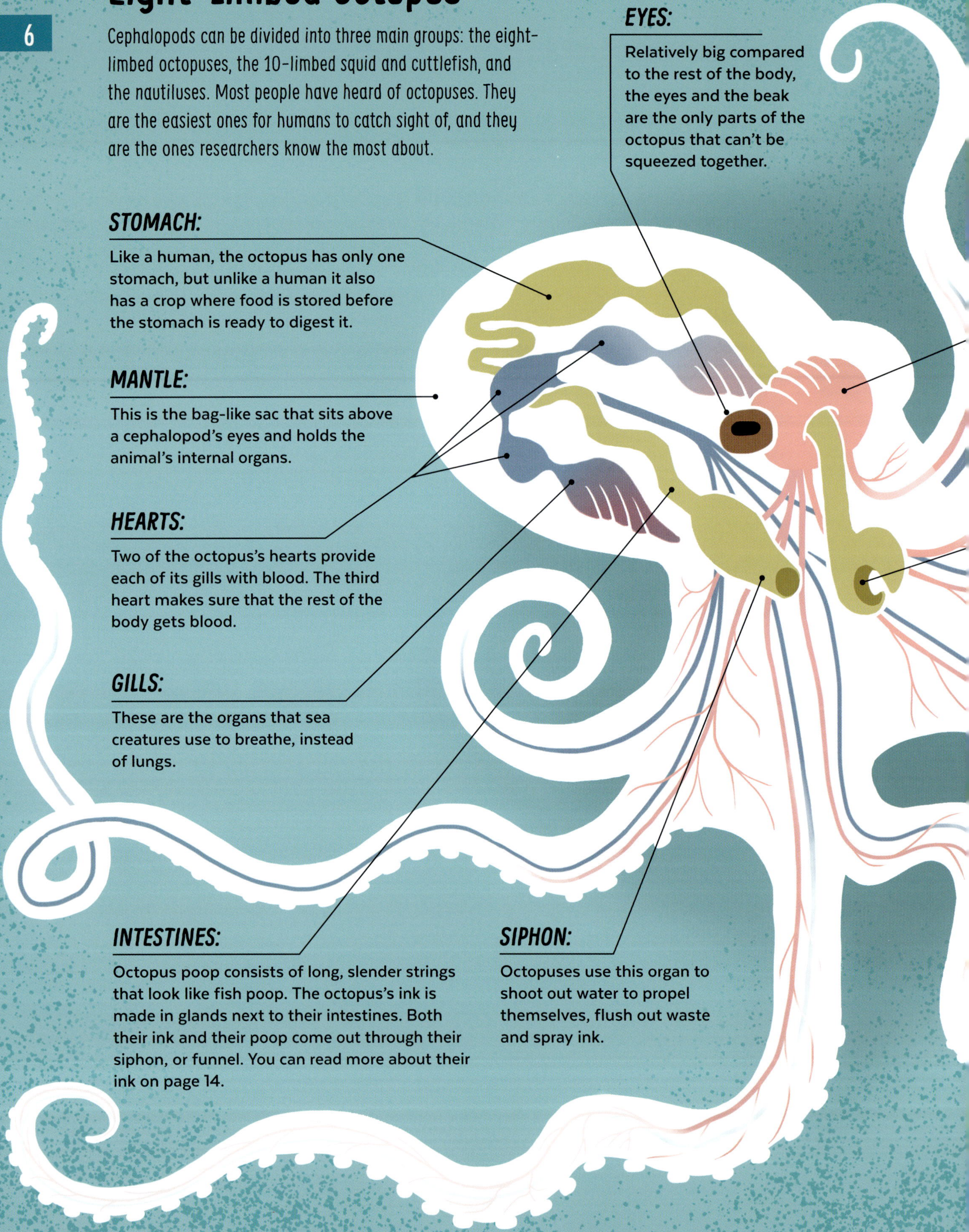

EYES:

Relatively big compared to the rest of the body, the eyes and the beak are the only parts of the octopus that can't be squeezed together.

STOMACH:

Like a human, the octopus has only one stomach, but unlike a human it also has a crop where food is stored before the stomach is ready to digest it.

MANTLE:

This is the bag-like sac that sits above a cephalopod's eyes and holds the animal's internal organs.

HEARTS:

Two of the octopus's hearts provide each of its gills with blood. The third heart makes sure that the rest of the body gets blood.

GILLS:

These are the organs that sea creatures use to breathe, instead of lungs.

INTESTINES:

Octopus poop consists of long, slender strings that look like fish poop. The octopus's ink is made in glands next to their intestines. Both their ink and their poop come out through their siphon, or funnel. You can read more about their ink on page 14.

SIPHON:

Octopuses use this organ to shoot out water to propel themselves, flush out waste and spray ink.

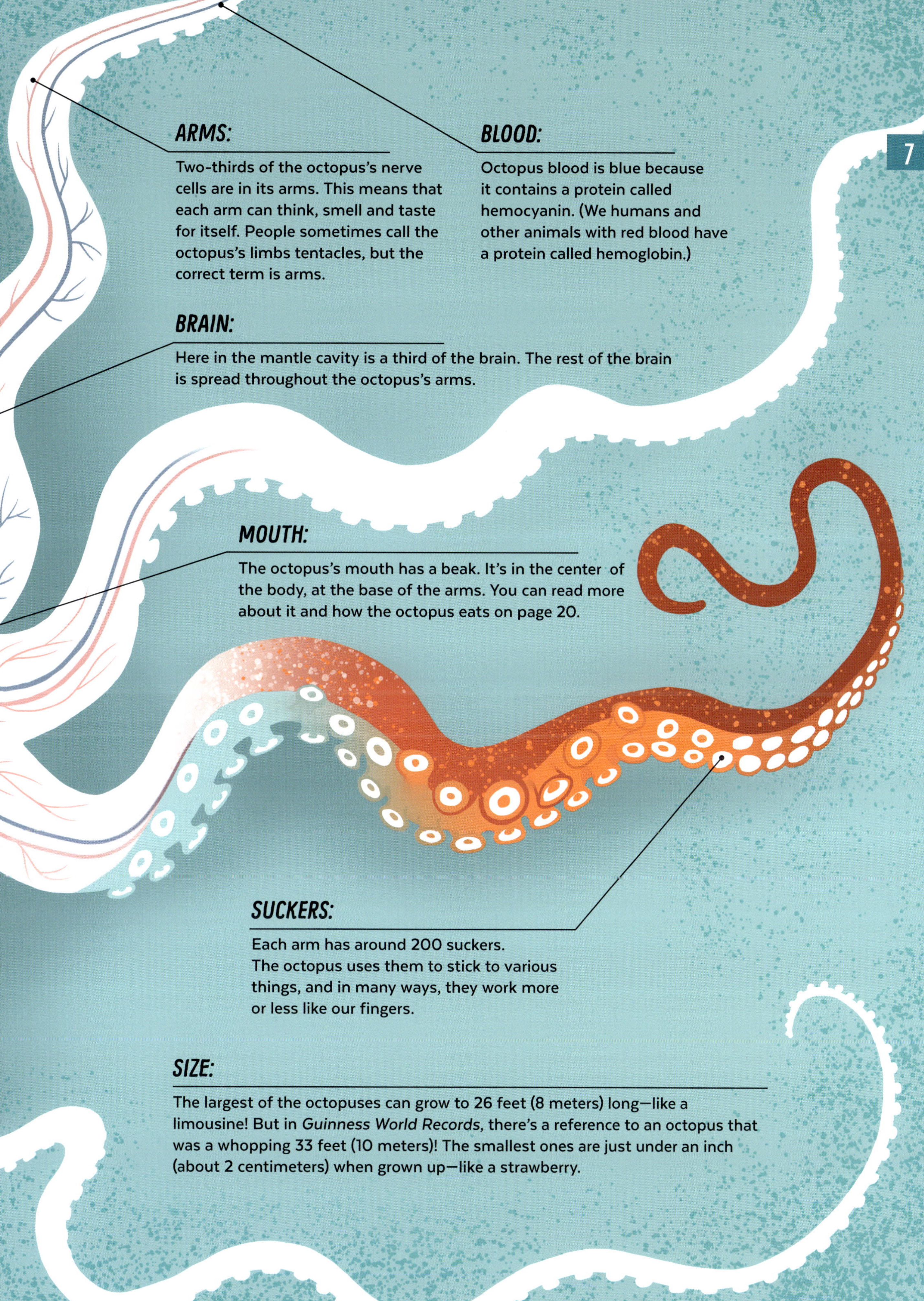

ARMS:

Two-thirds of the octopus's nerve cells are in its arms. This means that each arm can think, smell and taste for itself. People sometimes call the octopus's limbs tentacles, but the correct term is arms.

BLOOD:

Octopus blood is blue because it contains a protein called hemocyanin. (We humans and other animals with red blood have a protein called hemoglobin.)

BRAIN:

Here in the mantle cavity is a third of the brain. The rest of the brain is spread throughout the octopus's arms.

MOUTH:

The octopus's mouth has a beak. It's in the center of the body, at the base of the arms. You can read more about it and how the octopus eats on page 20.

SUCKERS:

Each arm has around 200 suckers. The octopus uses them to stick to various things, and in many ways, they work more or less like our fingers.

SIZE:

The largest of the octopuses can grow to 26 feet (8 meters) long—like a limousine! But in *Guinness World Records*, there's a reference to an octopus that was a whopping 33 feet (10 meters)! The smallest ones are just under an inch (about 2 centimeters) when grown up—like a strawberry.

Ten-Limbed Cephalopods

Much of what you have just read about the octopus is true for 10-limbed cephalopods too, which are technically called decapodiformes and include squid and cuttlefish. There are a few differences between them, however.

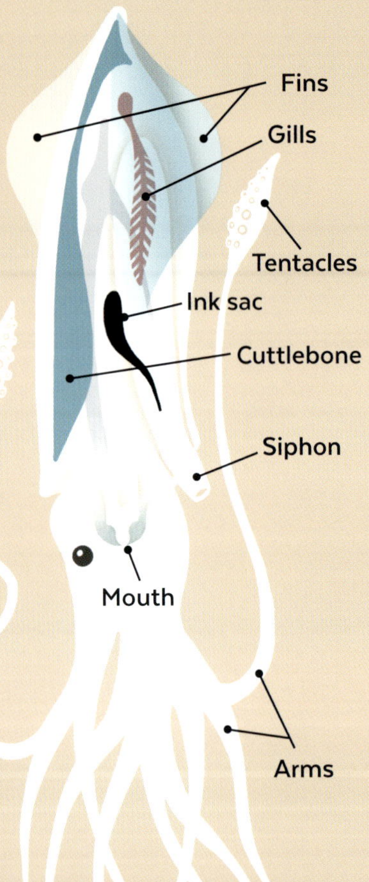

FINS: These make squid and cuttlefish good swimmers.

MANTLE: This part alone in decapodiformes can be as long as 13 feet (4 meters).

INTERNAL SHELL: Unlike octopuses, the decapodiformes have a thin internal shell, which is called a cuttlebone in cuttlefish and a pen in squid. After a squid or cuttlefish dies, these pens or cuttlebones can wash up onto the beach and be mistaken for shells.

LIMBS: Eight of their limbs are primarily used for swimming and movement. The two longer ones, called tentacles, have sharp hooks at the ends that are good for catching prey. The tentacles of the largest 10-limbed cephalopods can be up to 43 feet (13 meters) long.

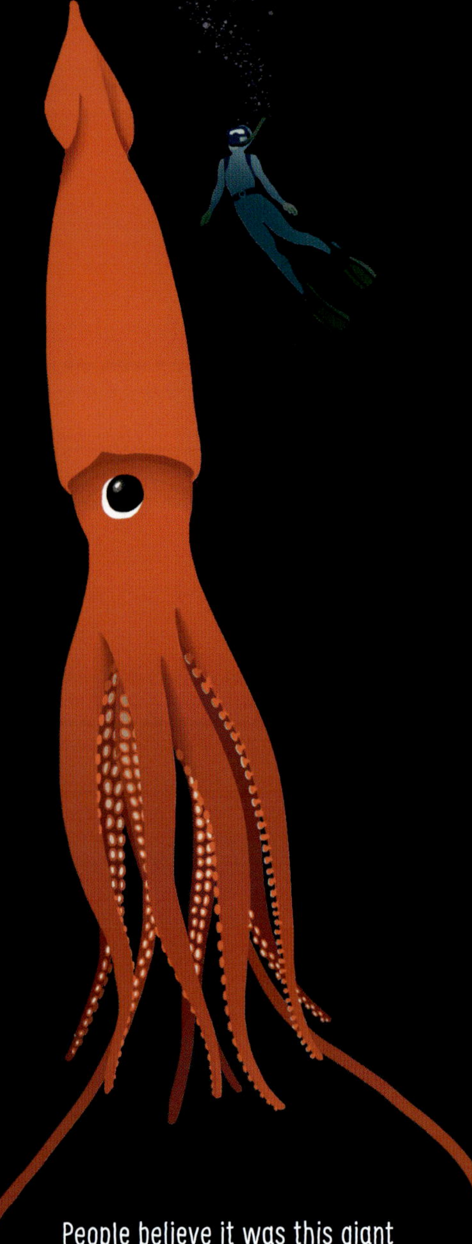

People believe it was this giant squid that inspired the legend of the kraken, a sea monster. In early times, sailors worried that the kraken would pull their ships down into the sea. But in reality, this cephalopod rarely comes to the surface. In general, it doesn't move much and therefore doesn't need more than 2 ounces (60 grams) of food per day, even though it's so big.

The world's largest squid has 10 limbs and is called the colossal squid. It can weigh around a ton and grow as long as 46 feet (14 meters). In other words, it's both taller and longer than a house or *Tyrannosaurus rex*! The colossal squid usually lives at depths of 1.2 miles (2 kilometers) or more, where it's totally dark. But it can see anyway, thanks to its eyes, which are as big as plates.

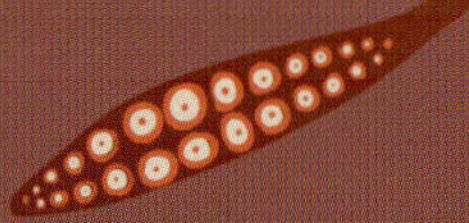

Nautilus

The nautilus is different in many ways from octopuses, squid and cuttlefish. For one thing, it lives longer, to around 20 years old.

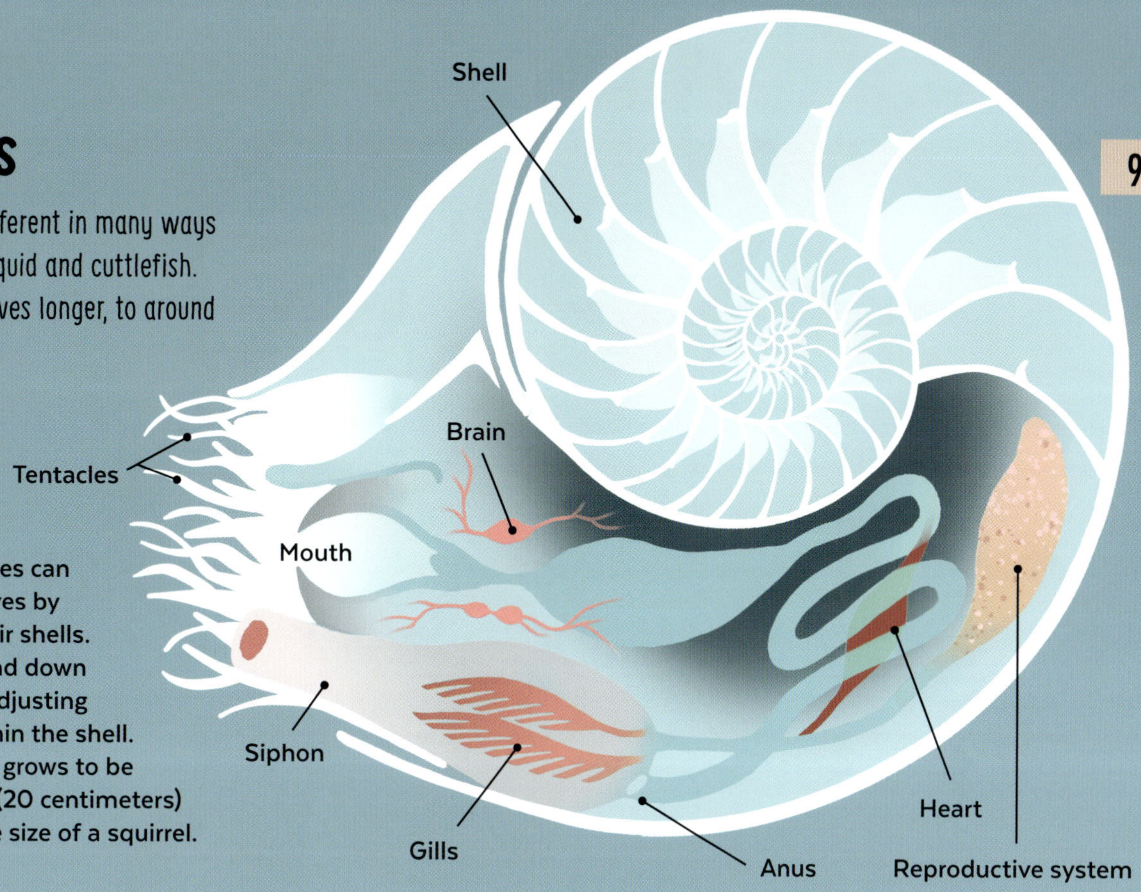

Shell
Tentacles
Brain
Mouth
Siphon
Gills
Anus
Heart
Reproductive system

SHELL: Nautiluses can protect themselves by creeping into their shells. They move up and down in the water by adjusting the pressure within the shell. The shell usually grows to be around 8 inches (20 centimeters) across, about the size of a squirrel.

LIMBS: They have 60 to 90 limbs usually called tentacles, but these limbs are not as long and powerful as those of the eight-limbed octopuses and 10-limbed squid and cuttlefish.

BRAIN: Nautiluses are not as intelligent and can't protect themselves or hunt in the same clever ways as the octopuses, squid and cuttlefish can, as you'll read later.

Human:
"Oh, imagine having eight limbs! I could do so many things at once!"

Octopus:
"Oh, imagine having 10 limbs! I could do so many things at once!"

Squid:
"Oh, imagine having 90 limbs! I could do so many things at once!"

Nautilus:
"Sigh. All these limbs keep getting tangled up. Imagine having only four limbs to keep track of!"

Cephalopods of the World

Scientists are always discovering new types of cephalopods. Right now they know of about 300 types, or species, of octopuses, 300 species of squid, 120 types of cuttlefish and 6 types of nautiluses.

DUMBO OCTOPUS
The dumbo octopus got its name because it looks like the Disney elephant Dumbo. It's not its ears that stick out, though, but its fins. This octopus doesn't have any ink because it doesn't need it. It lives 2 to 2.5 miles (3 to 4 kilometers) under the sea, and it's always dark there!

COCONUT OCTOPUS
The coconut octopus is a medium-sized octopus. When it walks along the seafloor, it usually uses just two of its legs. When it's not hiding in a coconut, it likes to dig down into the sand.

CUTTLEFISH
Cuttlefish are rounder and a little more ungainly than squid. They move more slowly and use their side fins to help propel themselves.

GLASS OCTOPUS
The glass octopus is almost completely transparent. The only parts you can't see through are its eyes and part of its digestive system.

BOBTAIL SQUID
There are four similar types—the common bobtail, the Atlantic bobtail, the stout bobtail and the warty bobtail. These cute cephalopods are small, just 1-3 inches (2-8 centimeters) as fully grown adults.

The Atlantic bobtail

GIANT PACIFIC OCTOPUS
The giant Pacific octopus is the largest of the octopuses. On average they weigh around 33 pounds (15 kilograms) and are 13 feet (4 meters) long as fully grown adults, but some have been found that weigh as much as 110 pounds (50 kilograms) or more.

CURLED OCTOPUS

This octopus is sometimes called the horned octopus or the northern octopus, but curled octopus is a good name because it keeps its arms tightly curled.

NAUTILUS

The nautilus has a hard shell that is divided into chambers, which are connected by a tube, or siphon. The creature itself lives in the largest of the chambers, and the others hold seawater and gas, allowing it to float and propel itself where it wants to go.

VAMPIRE SQUID

Vampire squids don't live off blood as you might think. They eat animal debris that falls toward the seafloor, including poop and corpses. When it isn't using its extra-long filament-arms to gather food, it stores them in a pocket in its mantle.

STRAWBERRY SQUID

The strawberry squid has a little blue eye and a big yellow one, which allows it to see well in different types of light below the surface. Its name comes from its red color and also its little spots that look like the seeds on strawberries.

MIMIC OCTOPUS

The mimic octopus is easily confused with the wunderpus octopus, which it looks very similar to. Besides camouflaging itself to blend with its surroundings, this octopus can also mimic other animals' behavior. For example, it can scare off predators by mimicking poisonous red lionfish and coral reef snakes.

BLUE-RINGED OCTOPUS

Watch out for this one! While most cephalopods have some kind of venom, the blue-ringed octopus is one of the few that is dangerous for people.

CASPER

This species was discovered only recently and hasn't been given a scientific name yet. It was named Casper after the little ghost in the Disney film of the same name.

BIGFIN REEF SQUID, or GLITTER SQUID

With the help of pigment cells (leucophores) in their skin, this squid can reflect the light so that it turns white in white light, green in green light and red in red light.

Ancient Animals

The cephalopods have existed on our planet for a long, long time. They were here before the dinosaurs. *Stenopterygius*, *Mosasaurus* and *Albertonectes*, among others, all thought cephalopods were a really tasty food.

When the great meteorite came, the one that hit Earth and killed the dinosaurs, the cephalopods survived. On land and near the surface of the sea, it got too warm for many animals, but cephalopods could swim so deep that they found cool enough water. Under the water, there was also food for them, even after the meteorite.

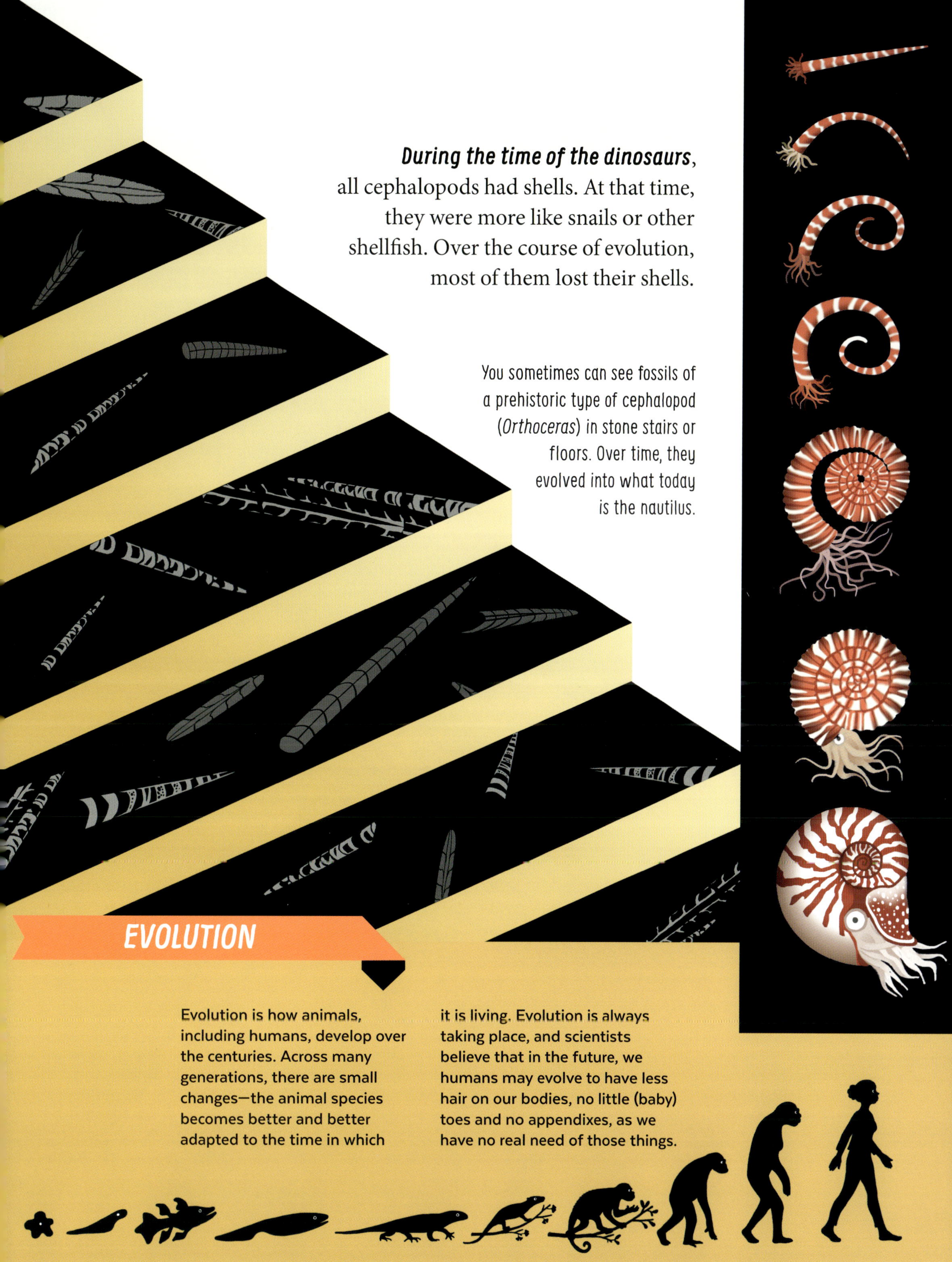

During the time of the dinosaurs, all cephalopods had shells. At that time, they were more like snails or other shellfish. Over the course of evolution, most of them lost their shells.

You sometimes can see fossils of a prehistoric type of cephalopod (*Orthoceras*) in stone stairs or floors. Over time, they evolved into what today is the nautilus.

EVOLUTION

Evolution is how animals, including humans, develop over the centuries. Across many generations, there are small changes—the animal species becomes better and better adapted to the time in which it is living. Evolution is always taking place, and scientists believe that in the future, we humans may evolve to have less hair on our bodies, no little (baby) toes and no appendixes, as we have no real need of those things.

Survival

Snails, crabs and nautiluses use their shells to protect themselves from predators who would otherwise easily eat them up. But what do the octopuses and squid and cuttlefish do to protect themselves? They also have lots of enemies who'd like to eat them—sharks, whales, larger octopuses, big fish and, of course, us humans. We are the biggest threat to cephalopods.

Cephalopods have a lot of smart ways to deter their enemies! They have their ink, the dark liquid they can shoot out so that it is hard for their predator to see them clearly. That gives them a chance to flee while their enemy's vision is limited.

Second, they can squirt out ink with a lot of mucus in it. This creates a gooey lump about the same size as the octopus or squid itself. It then looks like there are two of them, which confuses the enemy.

They also have a third clever survival tactic. If an enemy gets hold of one of their limbs, or if they get a limb stuck in something, cephalopods can let the limb go and still swim away. Losing a limb weakens them but often saves their lives. After just a few days, a new limb starts to grow in the same spot. Within a few months the new limb is fully grown.

Masters of Hiding

A fourth trick cephalopods use to hide from enemies is camouflage. They can camouflage themselves faster than any other animal on the planet. In less than a second they can change their color or shape and make their skin smooth, gnarled or lumpy.

With the help of camouflage, they can mimic different things in the water, such as a coral reef, a stone or a large piece of algae floating around. This makes it hard for many predators to discover them. And imagine how great they are at playing hide-and-seek!

Just below the surface of the skin of cephalopods there are cells that contain pigment and can reflect light. This feature allows them to swiftly change the color, pattern and structure of their skin. The cephalopod controls these cells by tensing or releasing the muscles the cells are in.

Some cephalopod species can even create their own light. They can shine this light on their own shadows, which is another way to hide. And for the cephalopods that live farthest down, in the darkest areas of the sea, this light is also good for attracting prey.

Camouflage is like pulling on an invisibility cloak. It makes you look so much like your surroundings that you can't be seen. There are some other animals that are good at camouflaging themselves, such as chameleons. Bush crickets, stick insects and other insects can also camouflage themselves, but not in the same way. They can't change color, but they always look like the environment they most often inhabit.

Humans camouflage themselves sometimes too. In the military, soldiers wear uniforms that can make them hard to see in forests, deserts or snowy landscapes.

DID YOU KNOW THAT...?

Soldiers want to be as good as cephalopods at camouflaging themselves. In the military, people are studying cephalopod skin and trying to develop uniforms with the same qualities.

Laurel and Heidi

Laurel lives in Alaska. One day when she came home from school, her dad, David, was waiting in the hallway, and he said he had a surprise for her. Her eyes lit up—she thought the moment had arrived when she was finally going to get a little dog, the pet she'd always wanted. Instead there was a gigantic aquarium in the living room. With an octopus* in it! Her father was a professor of marine biology, and he thought that this was a pet they'd both enjoy. He also thought that living with it would be a good way to study an octopus more closely!

In Alaska the water is cold, and the octopuses who live in the sea there move slowly. Professor David had seen a lot of those through his work, so he'd chosen an octopus from warmer waters farther south. It moved quickly back and forth in the aquarium. Laurel, who loved all animals and not just dogs, often stood there, watching the octopus. In the beginning, it mostly hid, so she called it Heidi, a play on the word *hide*.

Laurel was often home alone, as David worked in the field a lot. She would sit on the sofa and watch TV. When Laurel did that, Heidi would almost always lean against the side of the aquarium and train her eyes on the TV. Maybe octopuses like TV as much as people do.

Eventually Laurel spent more and more time with Heidi in the afternoons. Often she'd put her hand into the aquarium, and Heidi would stretch out an arm to greet her.

Heidi got braver and braver, and after a while she came over to Laurel and cuddled when she put her hand into the aquarium. They started to play together too. When Laurel dropped a plastic toy into the aquarium and it got pushed along by the water streaming from the purification filter, Heidi caught it. They did it over and over again. So even though Laurel didn't get a dog, she did still get to play fetch!

There's a documentary about Heidi, Laurel and David. It's called *Octopus: Making Contact*.

**Laurel's dad, David, is a scientist who studies marine life, and Heidi was part of his research. For most families, octopuses don't make good pets. They have quite short lives (only a couple of years) and, as wild animals, are happiest living free in the ocean. In some places it's even illegal to keep octopuses as pets.*

What Do Cephalopods Eat?

Cephalopods are predators. They hunt live prey such as fish, prawns, crabs, lobsters and snails. They can either fling themselves over their prey like a net or capture it with one or two of their limbs. In the middle of their body, at the base of their arms, they have a mouth with a sharp beak. With this beak they can crush the hard shells of crabs and snails. Some cephalopods also shoot a venom into their prey that breaks down its inner organs and makes it easy to swallow.

Cephalopod beaks are rock hard. They come out whole in the poop of predators that eat them.

Sometimes cephalopods steal what fishers catch. Crab fishers usually sink a cage down into the sea with a few prawns or other things crabs like. When the crabs smell the food, they hurry into the cages. But crabs aren't very intelligent, so once they're in, they're stuck and can't find their way out. When an octopus catches sight of the crabs in the cage, it slides in through one of the cage holes, eats the crabs and then is smart enough to quickly find its way out again.

When the crab fishers pull up the cages after a few hours, only empty crab shells are left…

Dangerous Cephalopods

Today we know that cephalopods don't usually pull boats down into the depths, but can they be dangerous for humans in other ways? Most cephalopods are harmless to us, but there are a few exceptions.

On the coast of Mexico, there is a gigantic squid called the Humboldt, also known as the red devil. It typically lives deep down, but sometimes this huge squid has floated into shallower waters and attacked people. Those who have been bitten have experienced terrible pain for a while but, luckily, haven't died.

Once a red devil tried to swallow an entire diver, but the diver managed to get free and survived.

The most dangerous cephalopod for humans is the blue-ringed octopus that lives along the coasts of Australia. The name comes from the blue rings that appear on its skin when it gets angry or scared. But usually it's sand-colored, which is good camouflage against the seafloor. It is only 4 to 8 inches (10 to 20 centimeters) long, but it has unusually large salivary glands, which contain a strong venom. People have died from bites from blue-ringed octopuses.

Where Do Cephalopods Live?

There are cephalopods in almost all the oceans and seas on the planet. But as they like salt water, they do not live in lakes. Nor are they found in the brackish waters of such places as the Baltic, Caspian or Black Sea.

Some species of cephalopods are found throughout the world, while others are more frequently found in certain locations.

FRESH WATER is in lakes and contains very little salt, less than 0.05 percent.

BRACKISH WATER is less salty than salt water, but saltier than fresh water. It has a salt content of between 0.05 and 3 percent.

SALT WATER occurs in seas and oceans. It contains a lot of salt, at least 3 percent and sometimes as much as 5 percent.

Some cephalopod species prefer shallower water while others live at depths of several thousand feet. Giant squid and nautiluses mostly live in really deep water, 2,000 feet (610 meters) or more below the surface. Nautiluses live only in warmer tropical water, like the Pacific Ocean and the Indian Ocean.

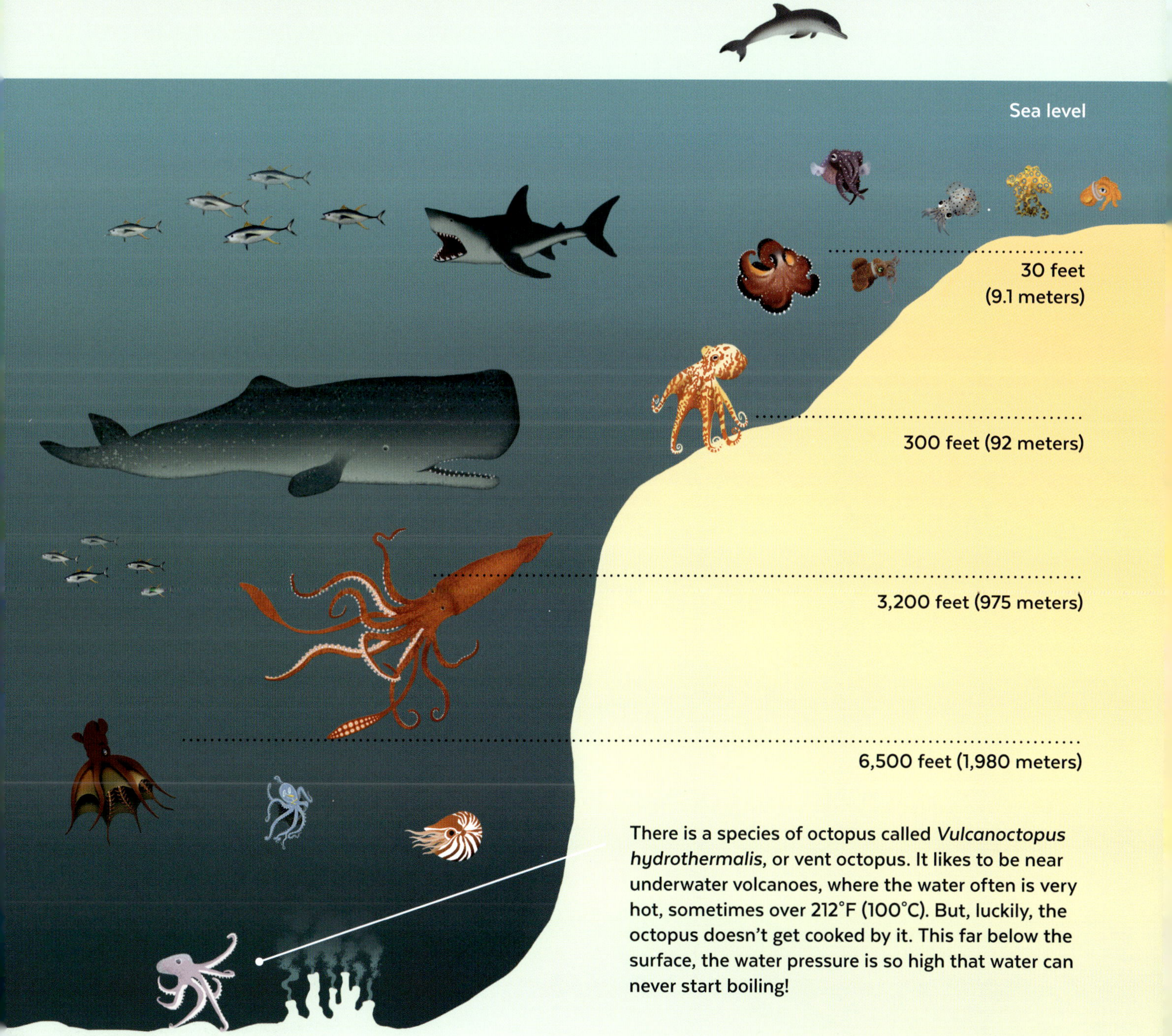

Sea level

30 feet (9.1 meters)

300 feet (92 meters)

3,200 feet (975 meters)

6,500 feet (1,980 meters)

There is a species of octopus called *Vulcanoctopus hydrothermalis*, or vent octopus. It likes to be near underwater volcanoes, where the water often is very hot, sometimes over 212°F (100°C). But, luckily, the octopus doesn't get cooked by it. This far below the surface, the water pressure is so high that water can never start boiling!

Intelligent Animals

Scientists have long wondered how smart cephalopods are, especially octopuses. So they've put them in aquariums and tested them by giving them different tasks. For example, they've been put in complicated mazes—and they've always found their way out.

Scientists have also tried to give octopuses food in a glass jar with a lid on it. It hasn't taken long for the octopuses to figure out how to unscrew the lid and get to the contents. Scientists have even discovered that when octopuses feel safe and full, they like to play, as Laurel saw with Heidi.

So the answer is simply that octopuses are really smart! Or at least as smart as dogs and cats.

ZOOLOGY is the study of all animals, including those on land. Both marine biologists and zoologists research octopuses.

MARINE BIOLOGY is the study of what lives in the sea. A marine biologist works to find out more about all the animals and plants in the sea and tries to protect the sea environment so that we humans don't destroy it.

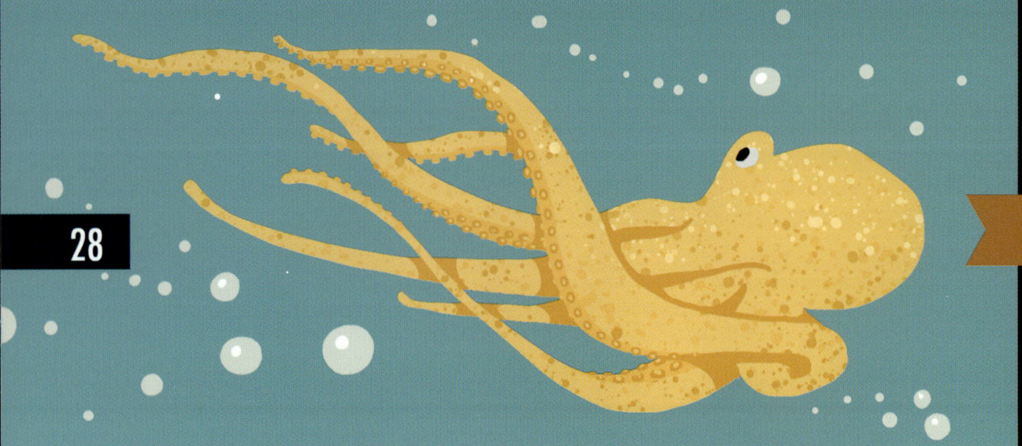

How Do Cephalopods Move?

Cephalopods move in several different ways. Octopuses can walk, climb and crawl on the seafloor. They can also get up onto land. They have gills and breathe underwater, but they can survive for a little while outside the water by getting some oxygen through their skin.

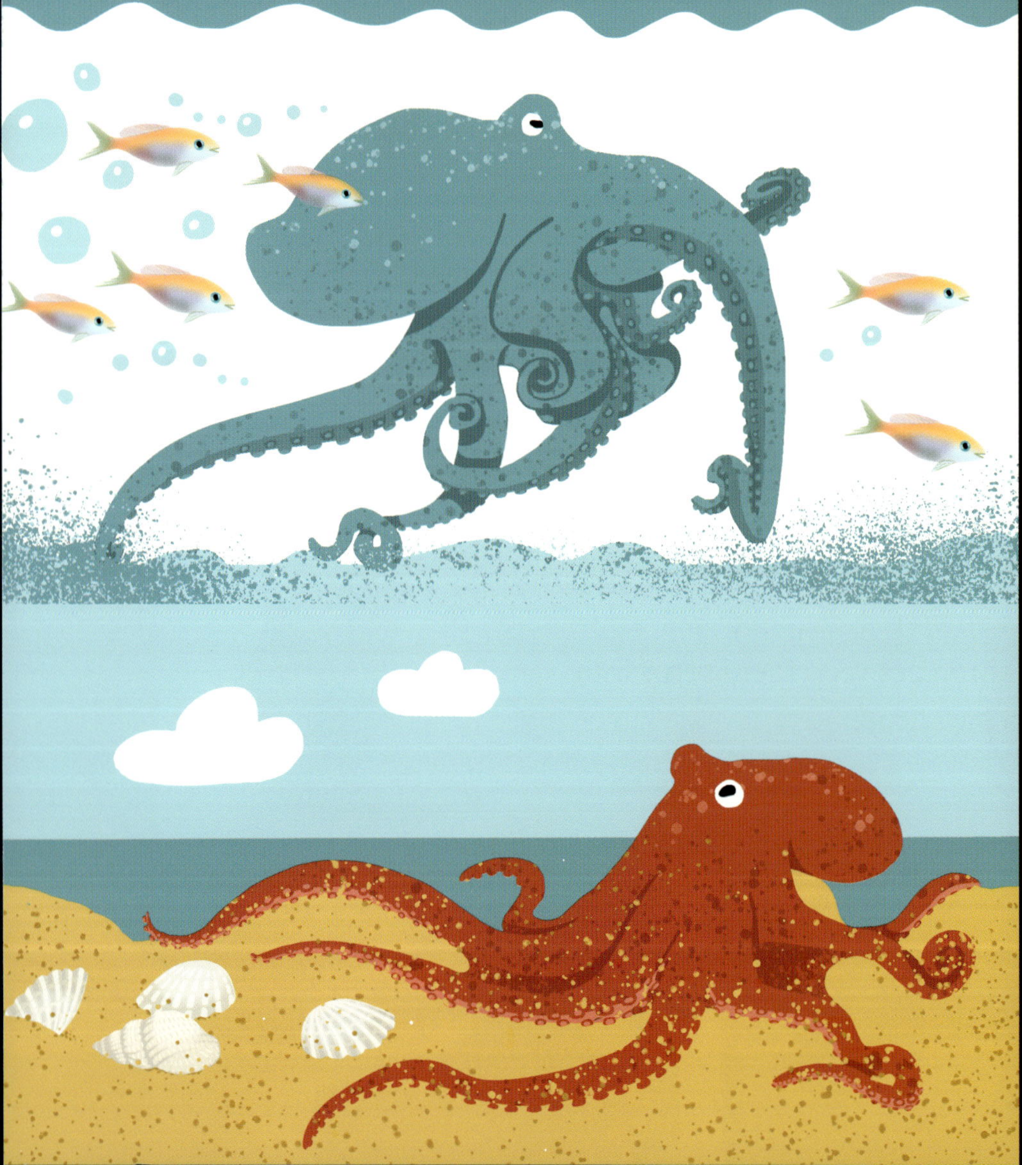

SWIMMING OLYMPICS

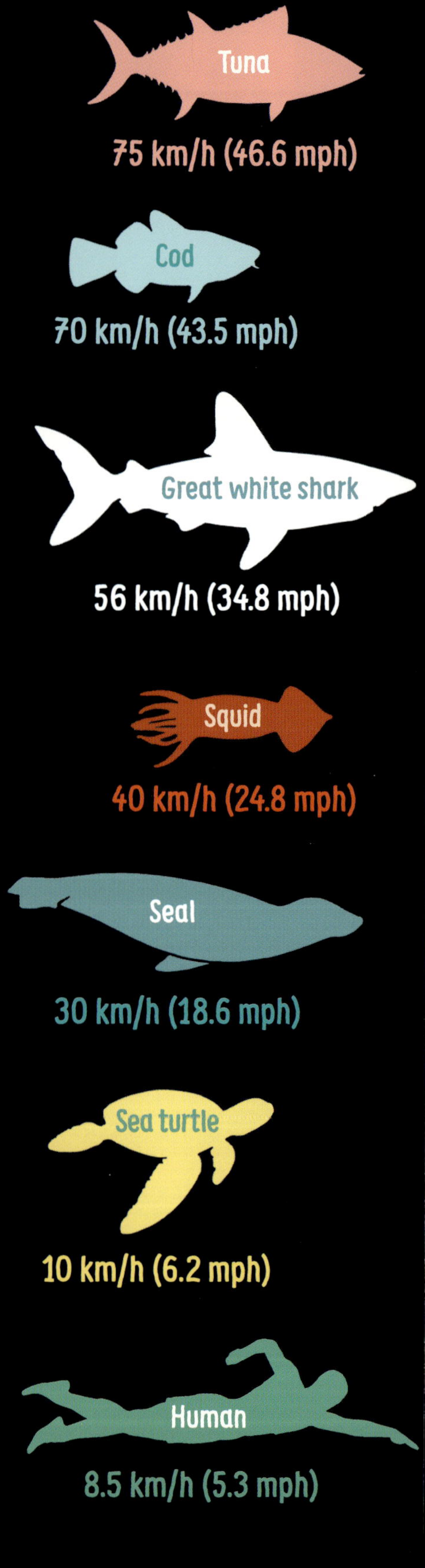

75 km/h (46.6 mph)

70 km/h (43.5 mph)

56 km/h (34.8 mph)

40 km/h (24.8 mph)

Seal

30 km/h (18.6 mph)

10 km/h (6.2 mph)

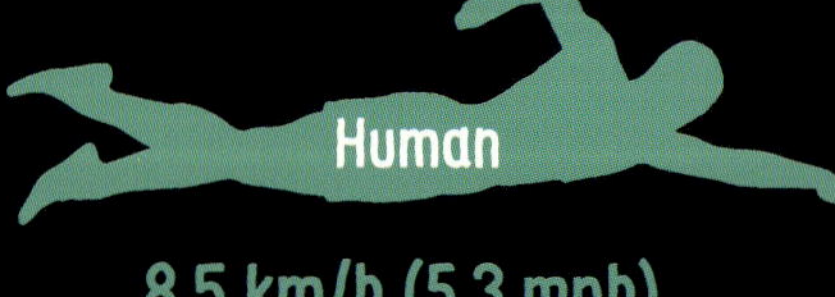

8.5 km/h (5.3 mph)

Squid use their fins to float and swim.

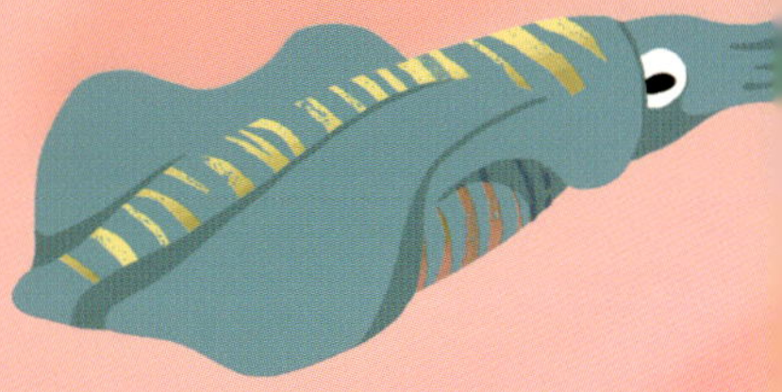

Both octopuses and squid can swim with the help of an inbuilt "jet engine." By contracting their mantle and pressing water out of their siphon, they can move at high speeds. They steer by aiming their siphon in different directions.

Some species can reach speeds of up to 36 feet (11 meters) per second. That's faster than Usain Bolt, who holds the world record among humans, running 328 feet (100 meters) in 9.58 seconds (34 feet/10.4 meters per second)!

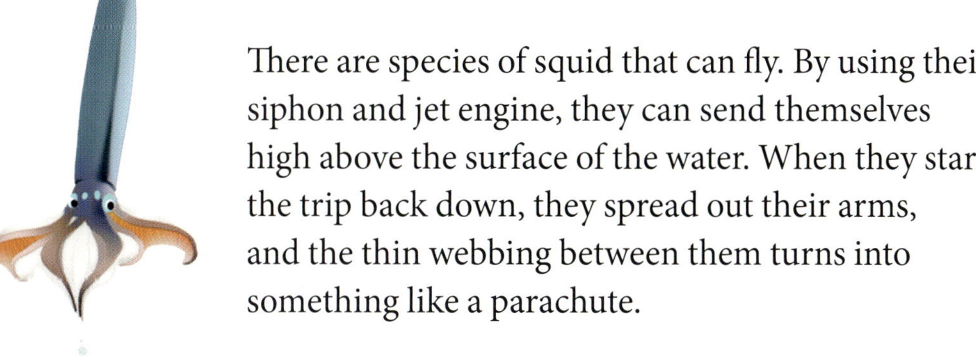

There are species of squid that can fly. By using their siphon and jet engine, they can send themselves high above the surface of the water. When they start the trip back down, they spread out their arms, and the thin webbing between them turns into something like a parachute.

When large squads of flying squid visit fishing communities, fishers need to watch out so they don't get a flying squid on their heads!

How Do Octopuses Have Babies?

Most octopuses reproduce only once. It usually happens right at the end of their life.

On a male octopus, one of their eight arms is also a kind of penis that contains sperm. When the male and the female meet, he puts this arm in her mantle and sends over his sperm. The male is usually very fast at putting his penis-arm into the female. Some species even leave the penis-arm there and swim away as quickly as possible.

And it's no wonder: sometimes the female eats the male if he hangs around!

The female then gets comfortable in a calm and protected spot, maybe in a rock crevice. She lays her eggs there. For some weeks she lies there, protecting her eggs and giving them oxygen by blowing water on them with her siphon. During that period, she neither hunts nor eats, and she loses a large portion of her body weight.

After a few weeks the eggs hatch, and hundreds or thousands of little octopuses swim out. By this time the mom octopus is weak and begins to die. The waves sweep her out of her nest, and, defenseless, she floats away on the current and is eaten by fish or other animals.

The little octopus babies have to manage on their own immediately, without any mom or dad. They must learn everything themselves, including how to stay safe and how to find food. Only a few of the newly hatched octopuses live to become fully grown. Many get eaten or can't find enough food.

DID YOU KNOW THAT...?

Octopuses lay different numbers of eggs depending on what species they belong to. The blue-ringed octopus lays "only" 50 to 100, while many other species lay up to 200,000 eggs at a time.

Preferably Alone?

Squid sometimes live in groups called squads, but cuttlefish, nautiluses and octopuses usually live alone. It's very unusual to meet more than one octopus at a time, and that's not surprising, because they sometimes eat one another. When scientists have tried to keep several such octopuses together in an aquarium, the animals have eaten one another up until only one octopus is left.

But in 2009 a diver in Australia found a place where 12 octopuses were living in close proximity. They seemed to communicate with one another, reach for each other and signal things among themselves by changing color. This place has been named Octopolis, which means octopus city.

In 2017 a similar place was found nearby, and it's called Octlantis. Scientists have placed underwater cameras there a number of times, but the octopuses quickly pull them loose and destroy them. So as of yet, we don't know why octopuses live together there but nowhere else.

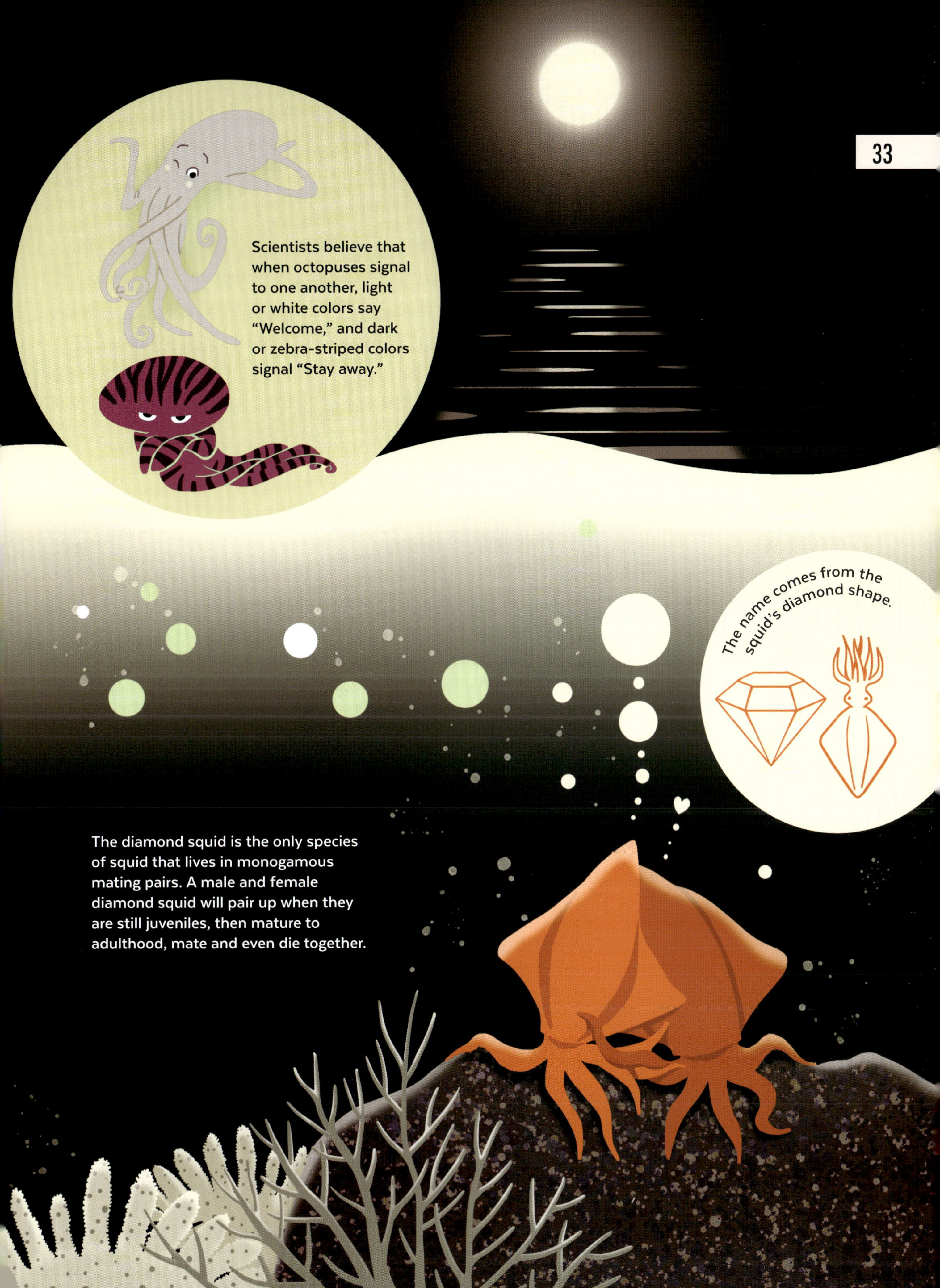

Scientists believe that when octopuses signal to one another, light or white colors say "Welcome," and dark or zebra-striped colors signal "Stay away."

The diamond squid is the only species of squid that lives in monogamous mating pairs. A male and female diamond squid will pair up when they are still juveniles, then mature to adulthood, mate and even die together.

My Octopus Teacher

The documentary filmmaker Craig Foster in South Africa had a unique way of getting to know an octopus. He began diving in the bay beyond his house every day for a year, and he studied the animals and the vegetation there. Every morning he put on his wetsuit, snorkel and mask, and dove in.

One day he saw a beautiful female octopus, which he watched from a distance. The next day he swam back to the same place and caught sight of her again. He began to do the same thing every morning, swimming around and searching until he found her.

She seemed to have settled in this bay, and she moved among different crevices and cozy hiding places she found there. Initially the octopus was scared of Craig. Then, slowly but surely, they began to get to know each other.

After about a month, the octopus would come and sit on Craig's outstretched hand. And gradually she came and sat on his upper body and let him stroke her.

Craig Foster made a documentary film about his relationship with the octopus. It's called *My Octopus Teacher*.

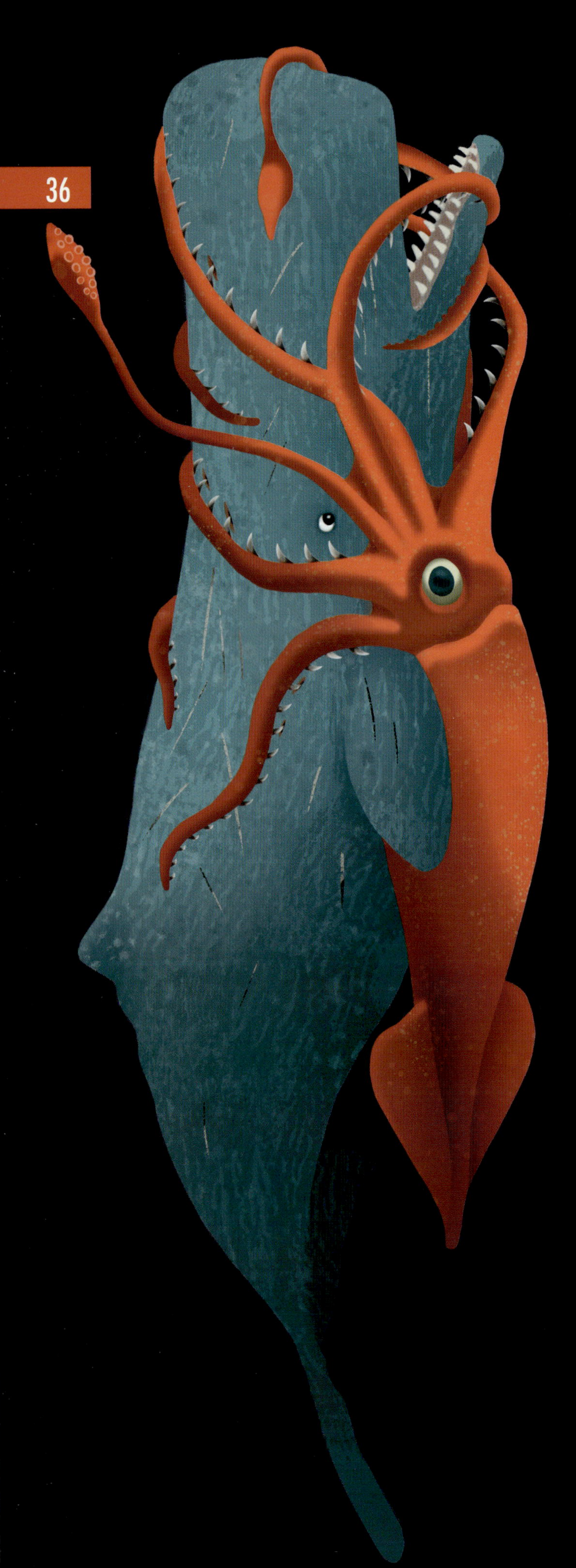

Fight!

Who do you think would win if a whale or shark and a cephalopod had a fight?

Large ocean predators like whales or sharks eat cephalopods, but cephalopods actually eat sharks too.

If a squid is little and a shark is big, the shark will usually win. But if they are around the same size, they can end up having real fights.

The shark has a very big mouth with lots of sharp teeth, and it is a very talented hunter. But the squid has its ink and its camouflage. And it has all those arms, which can capture the shark and hold it still. If a large cephalopod manages to get one of its strong arms around the shark's mouth, then it has a pretty good chance of winning the match.

Just as in the illustration to the left here, it's also not unusual to see scars on whales after they've fought with a squid. Both the suckers and the sharp hooks on the tentacles can leave marks.

Craig Foster, the photographer in South Africa, once saw his octopus buddy being hunted by a pyjama shark. First the octopus tried to hide by rolling into a ball with her arms over her sensitive head as protection. Then she pulled a bunch of shells over herself as camouflage and a shield. But the shark discovered her and attacked.

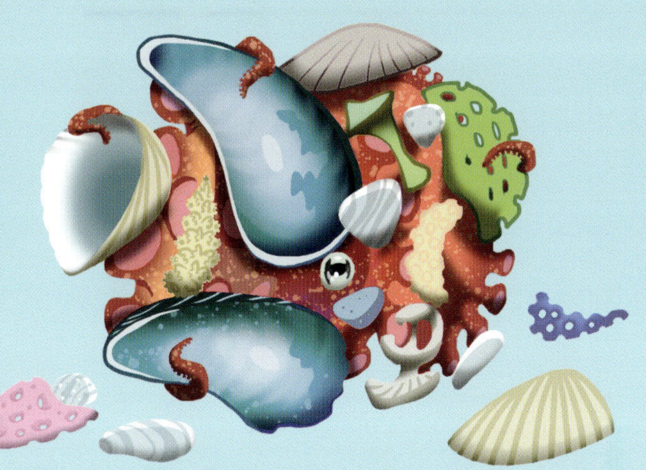

The octopus managed to crawl up onto the shark's back and hang on, protected as the shark spun around, unable to get at her. After a while the shark gave up and seemed to forget the octopus on its back. The octopus carefully let go and swam away in the other direction.

Ha ha, you weren't prepared for that!

DID YOU KNOW THAT...?

Just 1 percent of all the planet's animal species have been observed using tools. Among them are us humans, apes and some types of birds—but also octopuses. For example, they can hold up seashells as shields to protect themselves.

IN SPACE...

The cephalopod's immune system—the body's way of defending itself against illnesses—is similar to the human's. That's why the US National Aeronautics and Space Administration (NASA) recently sent 128 small squid up into space to study how they react and survive. Based on the results of this study, scientists hope that we can learn how to protect humans in space from illnesses.

The word octopus comes from the ancient Greek words for eight (oktō) and foot (pous).

8

There is a particular species of octopus called the coconut octopus. They use coconut shells to hide and live in. When they move, they always carry the shells with them.

Just a plain old camping trip!

Octopuses are strong. They can lift four times their own body weight! Compare that to an average male human, who can lift only their own body weight.

Octopuses even change color while they're sleeping. Scientists think this shows that they dream, just like we humans do.

ON THE PLATE...

As you already know, humans are the most dangerous animal for octopuses. All around the world, we capture and eat them. There are several different ways to fish for them: with a line, a trawler, a dart, a spear or a harpoon.

1. Around the Mediterranean, squid is usually eaten deep-fried with lemon juice squeezed on top. It's called calamari.

2. Many cultures include octopus in curries or stews.

3. Octopus is often served as sushi on top of a little cushion of rice.

1.

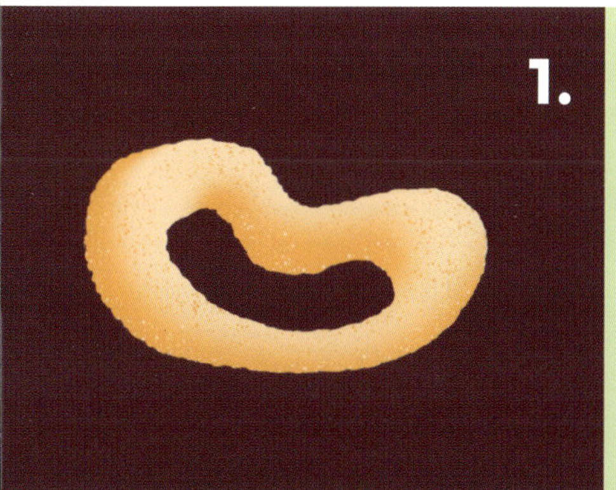

2.

3.

Oceans of the World
Greenland
Alaska
North America
The kraken
Laurel in Alaska
Mexico
Atlantic Ocean
Pacific Ocean
South America
The coconut octopus
The red devil
Craig Foster
N
W
E
S
The colossal squid

Arctic Ocean
In earlier times, people thought that the kraken lived here, in the waters between Norway and Greenland.
Europe
Asia
Pacific Ocean
Mediterranean Sea
The blue-ringed octopus
Africa
The nautilus
Oceania
South Africa
Australia
Indian Ocean
Octopolis—the octopus city
New Zealand
Inky the octopus
Antarctic Ocean
Antarctica

Index

aquariums, 4–5, 18–19, 26, 32
Atlantic bobtail squid, 10, 43
Australia, octopus city, 32

bigfin reef squid (glitter squid), 11, 43
blue-ringed octopus, 11, 23, 31, 43

camouflage, 16–17, 37
captivity, 4–5, 18–19
Casper octopus, 11, 24
cephalopods
- about, 3, 6, 9
- dangerous, 22–23
- diet of, 20, 21, 36
- distribution of, 24–25, 40–41
- prehistoric era, 12–13
- solitary lives, 32
- study of immune system, 38

coconut octopus, 10, 38, 43
color changes
- as communication, 23, 32, 33
- pigment cells, 11, 16

colossal squid, 8, 43
common bobtail squid, 10, 43
communication, with color, 23, 32, 33
crabs, 14, 20, 21
curled octopus, 11, 43
cuttlefish, 3, 8, 10, 43

deep ocean water zone, 25
defensive behaviors
- adaptations, 14–15, 28–29
- escape abilities, 3, 4–5, 28–29
- hiding ability, 16–17, 37, 38

diamond squid, 33, 43
dinosaurs, extinction, 12–13
dumbo octopus, 10, 24, 43

egg production, 30–31
escape abilities, 3, 4–5, 28–29

flying squid, 29
fossils, 13

giant Pacific octopus, 10, 24, 43
giant squid, 24, 25, 43
glass octopus, 10, 43

Heidi the octopus, 18–19, 26
humans
- attacks on, 22–23
- interactions with octopuses, 18–19, 21, 33–34
- use of cephalopods, 38, 39

humboldt squid, 22, 43
hunting behaviors
- and human interactions, 21, 22–23
- and prey, 16, 36
- techniques, 16, 20, 23

ink, cephalopod, 6, 14–15
Inky the octopus, 4–5
intelligence
- behaviors, 4–5, 21, 38
- testing, 26–27

life span, 5, 19
limbs, regrowth of, 15

marine biology, 18, 27
mating, 30–31, 33
mimic octopus, 11, 43
My Octopus Teacher (film), 33–34
myths, kraken, 2, 8, 41

nautiluses
- about, 3, 9, 11, 14, 25
- evolution of, 13
- types of, 10, 43

New Zealand, National Aquarium, 4–5

oceans
- deep ocean water zone, 25
- species distribution, 24, 40–41

octopuses
- defensive behaviors, 14–15
- as food, 39
- intelligence, 4–5, 26–27, 38
- life span, 5, 19
- playfulness, 18–19, 26
- reproduction, 30–31, 33
- size, 7
- social behavior, 32, 33
- structure, 3, 6–7, 28–29

Octopus: Making Contact (film), 18

predators, 14–15, 16, 36, 37
prehistoric era, 12–13
prey, 16, 20, 21, 36

sea monsters, 2, 8, 41
sharks, 14, 36, 37
shells
- nautiluses, 3, 9, 13, 14
- squids and cuttlefish, 8

skin, 11, 16, 28
speed and flexibility, 3, 28–29
squids
- defensive behaviors, 14–15
- flying, 29
- as food, 39
- giant, 8, 22, 36
- social behavior, 32, 33
- structure, 3, 8, 28, 29

stout bobtail squid, 10, 43
strawberry squid, 11, 24, 43

vampire squid, 11, 24, 43
venom, 20, 23
vent octopus, 25, 43
volcanoes, underwater vents, 25

warty bobtail squid, 10, 24, 43
whales, 14, 36
wunderpus octopus, 11, 43

zoology, 27

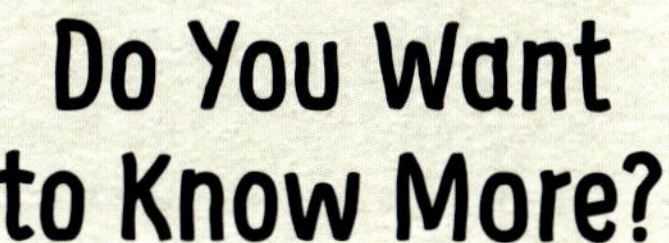

Do You Want to Know More?

If you want to know more about a particular cephalopod, try googling its scientific name!

Atlantic bobtail squid—*Sepiola atlantica*

Bigfin reef squid—*Sepioteuthis lessoniana*

Blue-ringed octopus—*Hapalochlaena* genus

Coconut octopus—*Amphioctopus marginatus*

Colossal squid—*Mesonychoteuthis hamiltoni*

Common bobtail squid—*Sepietta oweniana*

Common cuttlefish—*Sepia officinalis*

Curled octopus—*Eledone cirrhosa*

Cuttlefish—Sepiida family

Diamond squid—*Thysanoteuthis rhombus*

Dumbo octopus—*Grimpoteuthis* genus

European flying squid—*Todarodes sagittatus*

Giant Pacific octopus—*Enteroctopus dofleini*

Giant squid—*Architeuthis dux*

Glass octopus—*Vitreledonella richardi*

Humboldt squid (aka the red devil)—*Dosidicus gigas*

Mimic octopus—*Thaumoctopus mimicus*

Nautilus—Nautilidae family

Stout bobtail squid—*Rossia macrosoma*

Strawberry squid—*Histioteuthis heteropsis*

Vampire squid—*Vampyroteuthis infernalis*

Vent octopus—*Vulcanoctopus hydrothermalis*

Warty bobtail squid—*Rossia palpebrosa*

Wunderpus octopus—*Wunderpus photogenicus*